POLITICS OF THE WORLD

NO MORE BORING HISTORY!

HIMANK MITTAL

Contents

Preface

Our goal is to make you more knowledgeable so that you get smart. Schools make somethings boring so if history is someone's passion after going to school it will be ended. Because they only say to learn names of ancient people. But that's not real history. There is 1 fun activity at the end of the book and one very easy Question-answers sheet and 5 chapters. If you read it 200 days and learn everything in the timeline your talent is knowledge like me. It has explanation that makes the hardest thing to learn easy. It improves the power of reading. 5+ can easily understand it. The book has been made with checking of all data. It is made in India. And all creators are Indian. This book is not to disrespect any country. It is written in Ms word. Hope you enjoy the book!!

ch – history

russhian empire

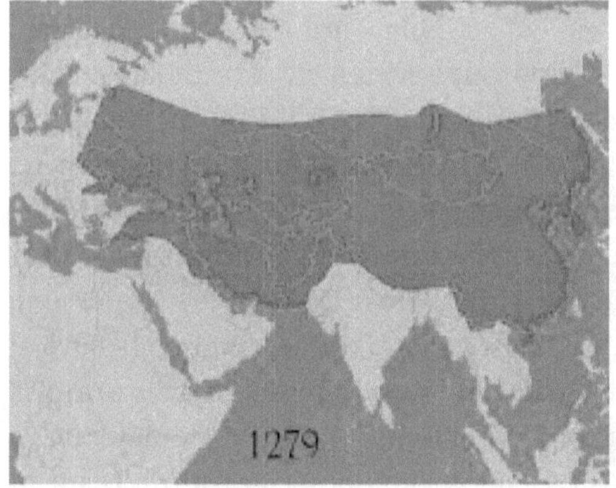

mongolian empire

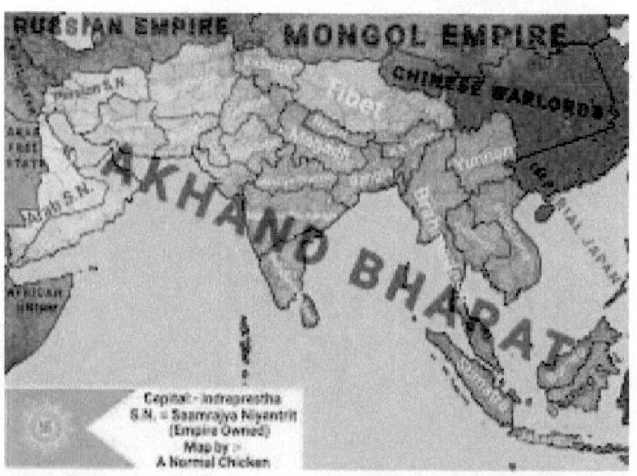

undivided india or as said akhand bharat

Suez canal is one of the most important canals. It connects middle east with Europe and Africa with Europe and Indian ocean countries with Europe. The second is Panama canal that helps ships from all 5 continents leaving south America and north America to Alaska(USA).the world's most powerful country. There are many more. Many years ago Asia was divided into three parts. Russian empire Mongolian empire and undivided India. In Russian empire todays Ukraine, Belarus, Germany, Poland and the Baltic states come. in Mongolia China, Pakistan, middle east, Mongolia Asian east come. In India south India comes. The last religion was Sikh and oldest was Hinduism. In the world there are 195 countries. 10 countries are not recognized. So total is 205 countries. World trade hub is China. But almost all world hate China. Allies of China are Russia, Pakistan, Iraq,Jordan,Syria,Lebanon,iran,kyrgistan,Uzbekistan etc. The most enemies are USA, India, Canada almost all Europe all NATO Taiwan, Mongolia. Russia has also enemies like all NATO, EU Ukraine, Finland, Sweden hate. There are also superpowers the top four are USA,CHINA,RUSSIA,INDIA and all are nuclear powered countries. The can destroy the world by only one command. World biggest army with CHINA.USA is the worlds one of the most important countries . Russia and Ukraine almost all Europe is dependent on Russia for fuel and sunflower oil. All of the world is dependent for grain on Ukraine. But Ukraine has the least literacy rate in Europe. Russia has the biggest land. While Indonesia has most Islam in there country. Most Hinduism is in India.one time USA started ww3 with Cuba and soviet union. But the issue was solved. The most powerful thing is aircraft carrier in the ocean. It is with only 13 countries. USA has the most with 11 an 1 in manufracturing.. It was invented in China. It has power to light a whole city for a week. It has fighter planes. Destroyers, blasters , canals , it can't sink by a tsunami because it is taller than 9 feet's. If water comes in any compartment is can't spread. If fire catches it will stay in that compartment only. If someone tries to do air attack ship gets the message 12 km away. Then it can shot it. India has 94 unicorn staters more than united kingdom. Company with more worth than 1 billion dollars are called unicorn starters. First Africa was a colony of Europe. The world centre is London the capital of united kingdom. And ends in nowhere of Antarctica. Sweden claims 70% of Antarctica and 30% is unclaimed. The world wars where only between 1900 to 1950 and the war point was Europe and the rest allies. There is only one time nuclear bomb used by USA on Japan Hiroshima and Nagasaki. A city in Japan capital Tokyo. But also now the are allies. Most English speakers are in USA. Second is in India.

CHAPTER TWO

EMPIRES

In 30 December, 1922 soviet union was found .It collapsed in 25 December 1991.It was bigger than the surface area of Pluto. It included more than 12 countries and the capital was Moscow. It had fighted world war two and won. It had allies like India, China ect. It had fought cold war. It was a pretty powerful. But they can't control this much countries. Because of rebellions as they had captured so many countries. But soviet union can't be made today as Europe is now centralized and have made Nato,ueropean union. And now is pretty strong. Because of cold war computers were invented. They are one example of empires falling. One famous example is the British empire, French empire, Spanish empire, or the Mongolian empire.

PART 1:BRITISH EMPIRE

British empire started in the late 1500 BC and ended over 1 July 1997 because honking left the empire. They invaded Gaul, northern France the first invasion. It reached its peak in 1914 and a dialogue Got famous. "sun never sets in Britain as in India if its day in Australia it is night. But after fighting 2 world wars they had no money to handle their colonies. And colonies took advantage of it and rebelled. And this is how british empire was destroyed.

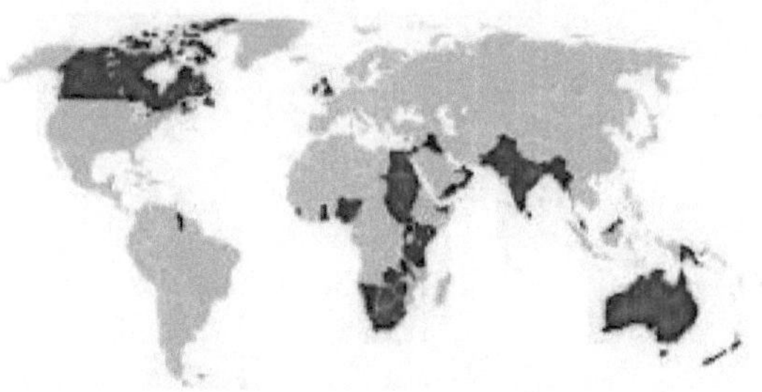

british empire

PART 2:FRENCH EMPIRE

French empire started in may 1804 and ended during the second ww2 when they were attacked from every where. It at its peak apex

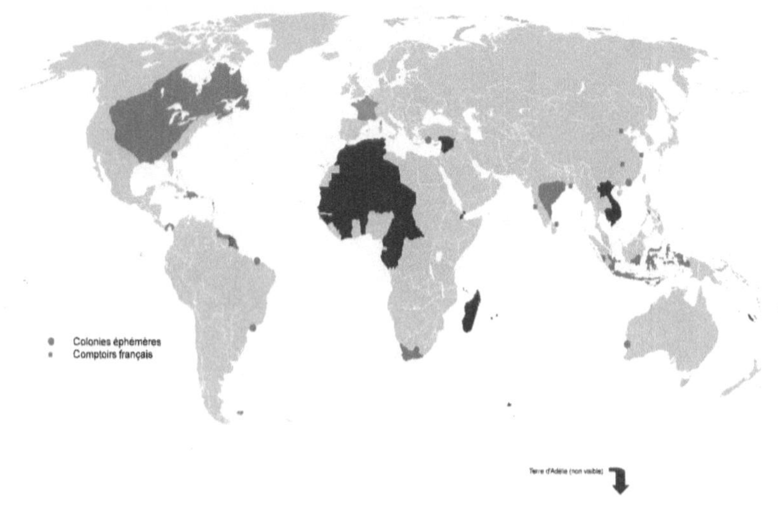

french empire

Between 1920 and 1930. It was also a big empire.

PART 3:SPANISH EMPIRE

17 April 1492 Spanish empire was borned.it was one of the biggest empires in the history. It collapsed in 1976.

spanish empire

Because people people started to protest for independence. It was at its peak in the 18th century and became the first empire to set as the sun sets in Spanish empire.it was very successful.

CHAPTER THREE

Borders of the world

Well, do you see borders like this,

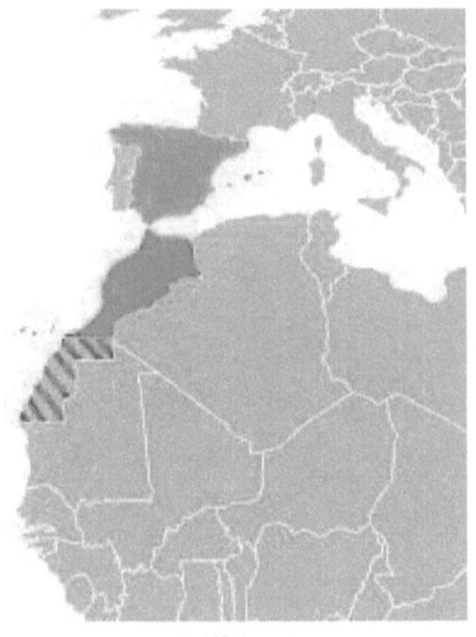

map you see

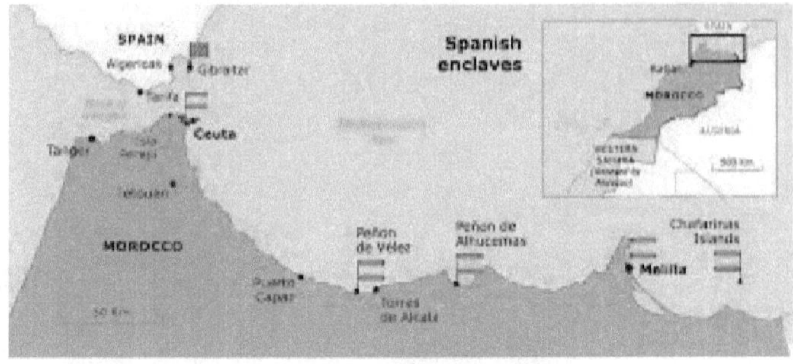

reality

World borders are not simple as shown in the maps, because when empires ended, they left countries weak and borders filled with conflicts. Like India- Pakistan by the British. Africa by European countries and some conflicts because of claims. eg-United kingdom and Ireland,India and china,UAE and Oman ect. ***world map size*** world map also doesn't shows the real size of contries. world map shows greenland 15 *bigger than africa but reality is the apposite.india is bigger than europe(excluding russia).and russia is bigger than the surface area of pluto.you can also search the true size of.com website on google to know more about it. the world map we see nowadays was made for sailors to use.

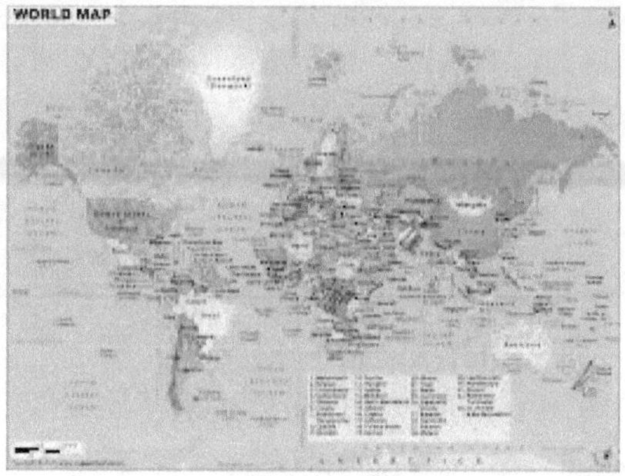

world map we see

CHAPTER FOUR

QUESTION-ANSWERS

Q1. Give one word answer.

1. Name one space agency-...............
2. Which country has the most aircraft carrier-..............

Q2. state true or false.

A. India has the most English speakers [ ]
B. Anti ballistic missile can destroy a missile [ ]
C. India has 94 unicorn businesses [ ]
D. World trade hub is China [ ]

Q3. Answer in some words.
Where was world 1 nuclear missile was launched? Why it was launched?

....

....
List some important canals?

....

CHAPTER FIVE

Computers

The first computer was invented by Charles Babbage (1822) but was not built until 1991! Alan Turing invented computer science. computers are a e

fun activity

draw the map of french empire and british empire together

Enter Caption

Ending

Our goal is to make you more knowledgeable so that you get smart. Schools make somethings boring so if history is someone's passion after going to school it will be ended. Because they only say to learn names of ancient people. But that's not real history. There is 1 fun activity at the end of the book and two very easy Question-answers sheets and 8 chapters.

<u>***The knowledgeable book***</u>

No boring history!!

Only interesting ones!!

Enjoy our book